MY FIRST
CHRISTMAS
High Contrast Baby Book

This Book Belongs To:

_____

_____

INSTRUCTION

HOW OFTEN SHOULD YOU VIEW THE BOOKS?

Do it every day. Show your child for at least a few minutes every day. "Watch as much as you can."

HOW LONG SHOULD CHILDREN LOOK AT BLACK AND WHITE CARDS?

Let your child focus on the picture for a short time, no longer than 30 seconds at a time.

MOTOR DEVELOPMENT - HAND-EYE?

Encourage your child to reach for the card and examine it with their hands.

ENJOY THE GIFT INSIDE

https://bit.ly/*********

THE GIFT IN PAGE 9

✳✳*✳*✳*✳*✳*

HELLO THERE, LITTLE ONE!

Are you ready for a Christmas adventure with Baby Santa? We will have so much fun exploring shapes in a snowy world!

SO, LET'S GOOOOOO!

HIGH CONTRAST + SIMPLE SHAPES =

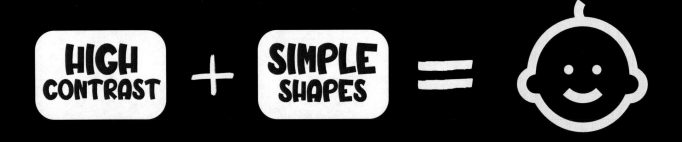

TA-RAAAAAA!!

🎁 🎁 🎁

HERE IS YOUR GIFT:

https://bit.ly/
4f4YOoW

TAP THIS LINK IN THE BROWSER AND ENJOY!
IF YOU LOVED THE BOOK AND THE GIFT GIVE US

⭐⭐⭐⭐

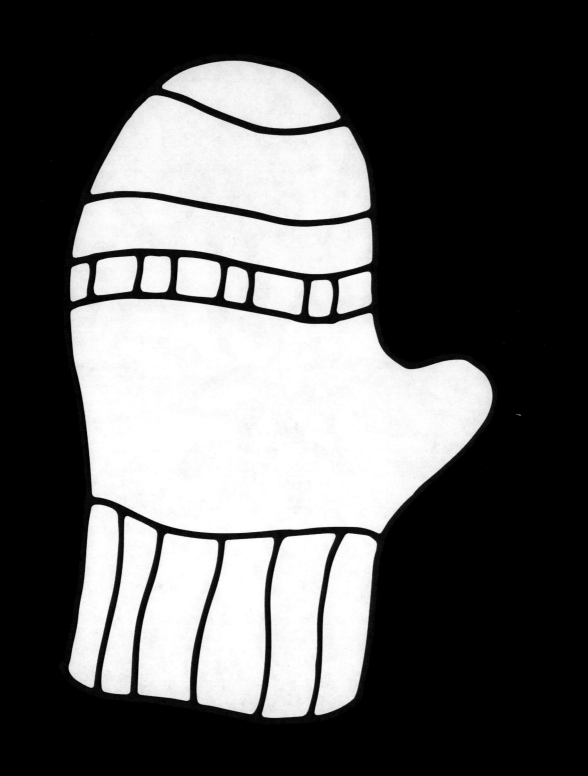

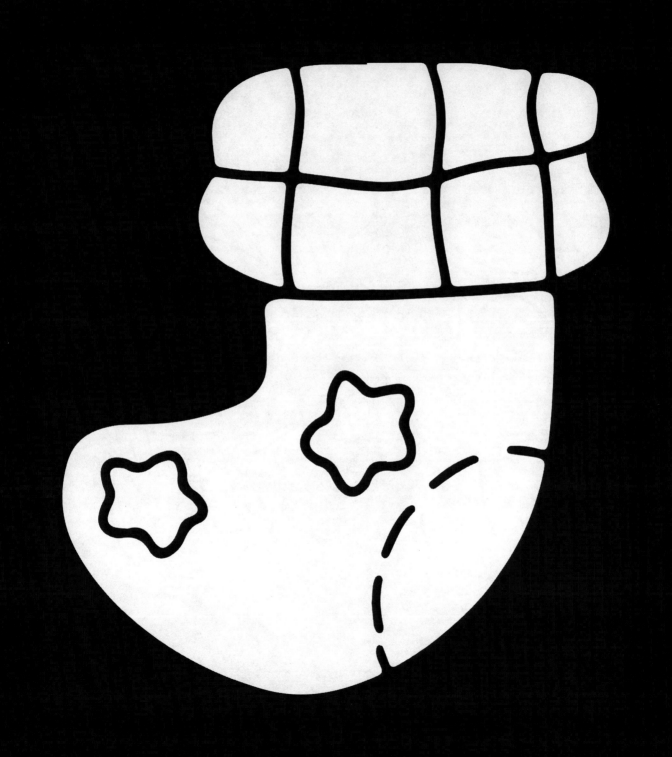

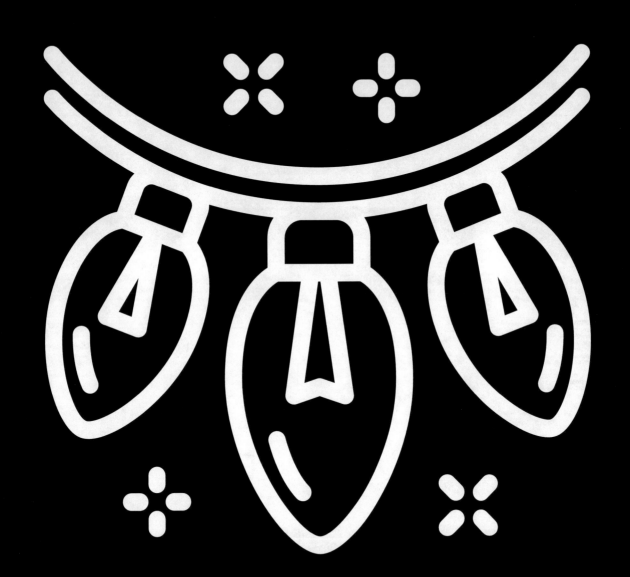

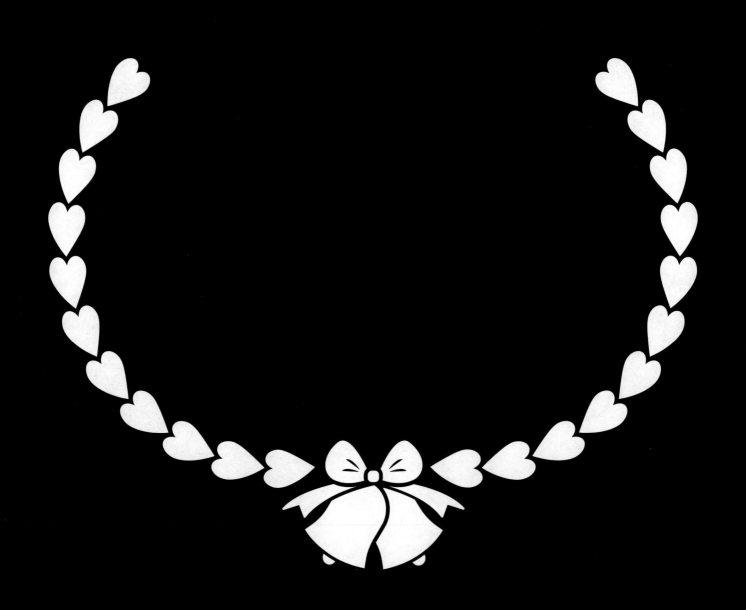

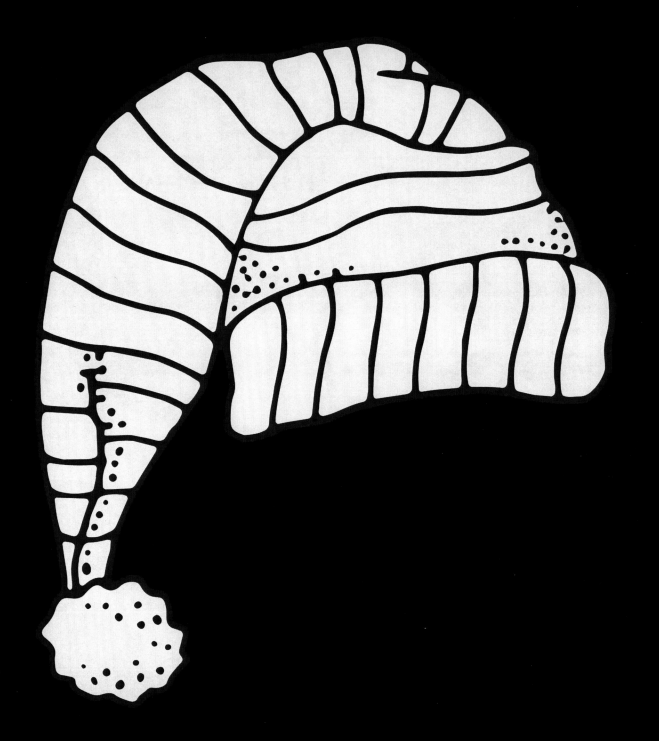

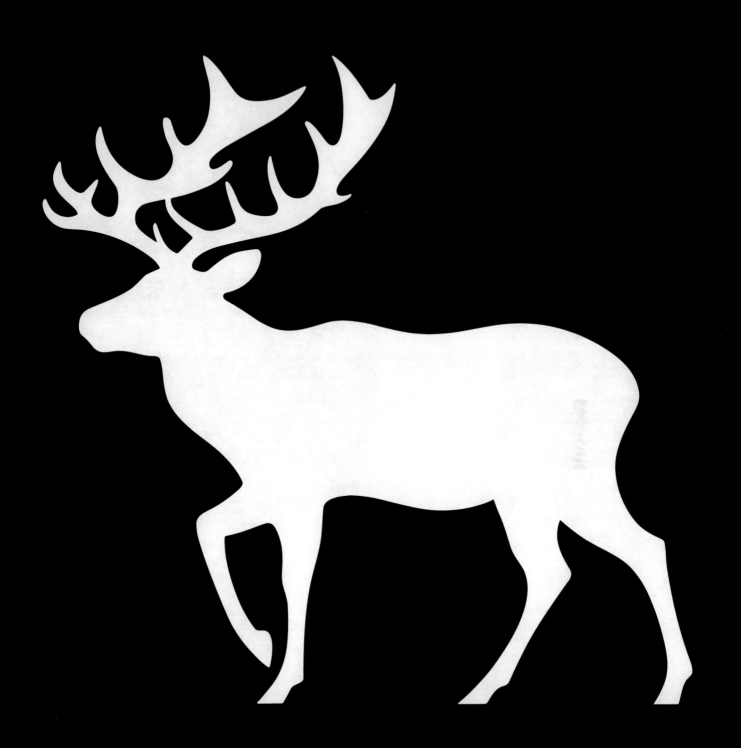

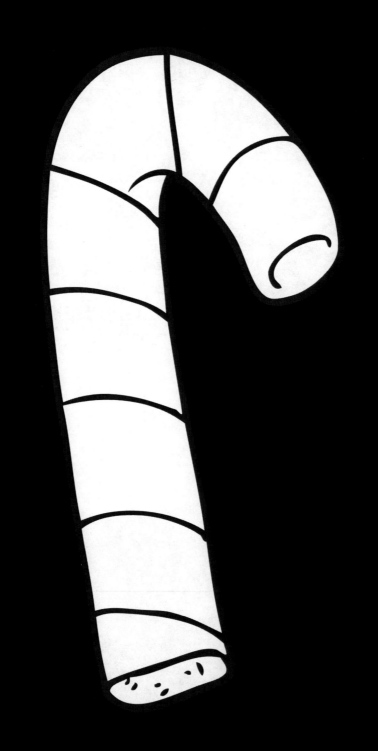

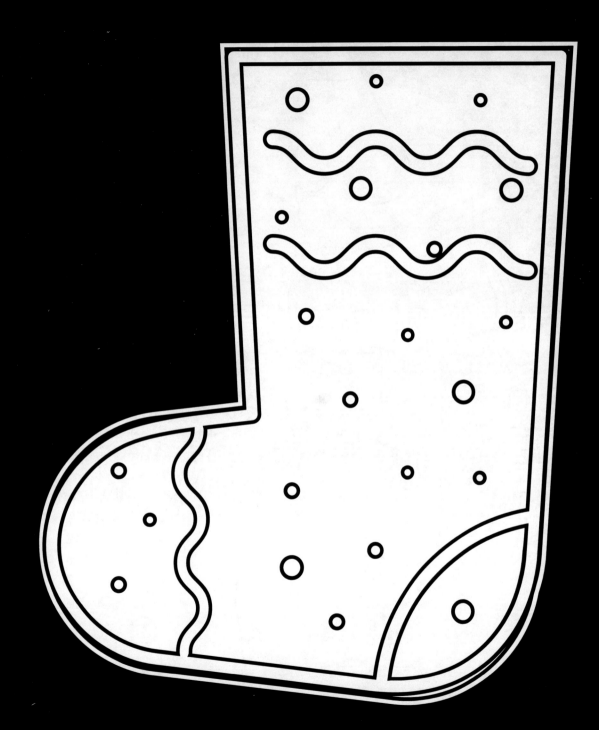

10740820R00059